J. Z. Butler, Howard Crosby

The Catskill Mountains, Pine Hill and Summit Mountain

J. Z. Butler, Howard Crosby

The Catskill Mountains, Pine Hill and Summit Mountain

ISBN/EAN: 9783743338883

Manufactured in Europe, USA, Canada, Australia, Japa

Cover: Foto ©Andreas Hilbeck / pixelio.de

Manufactured and distributed by brebook publishing software
(www.brebook.com)

J. Z. Butler, Howard Crosby

The Catskill Mountains, Pine Hill and Summit Mountain

1883

THE CATSKILL MOUNTAINS,

PINE HILL

-and-

SUMMIT MOUNTAIN;

BY

Rev. J. Z. Butler, D.D.,

Rev. Howard Crosby, D.D.,

And Others.

ILLUSTRATED BY DU BOIS P. HASBROUCK.

Rondout, N. Y.

Printed by Ye Kingston Freeman Company.

1883.

The Gateway of the Catskills,

VIA RONDOUT.

ULSTER & DELAWARE R. R.

Through the most Picturesque Region in America.

Famous Summer Resorts among the

CATSKILL MOUNTAINS.

This Route passes through the SHANDAKEN VALLEY and over the CATSKILL MOUNTAINS at
PINE HILL, and abounds in Magnificent Mountain Scenery,
Unrivaled for its Grandeur and Beauty.

THE ULSTER & DELAWARE RAILROAD,

In Connection with River and Rail Lines, forms the Shortest, Quickest and

Most Desirable Route

From New York City

To the Many Points of Interest in the CATSKILL MOUNTAIN REGION of Ulster, Greene,
Schoharie and Delaware Counties.

THROUGH TICKETS Sold at the Principal Eastern and Southern Cities.

CONNECTIONS: At RONDOUT, with Night Line Steamers from Pier 41, North River,
New York ; via RHINEBECK, with Day Line Steamers, N. Y. Cent. & Hud. River and
Hartford & Conn. W. Railroads ; via KINGSTON, with N. Y., L. Erie & Western and N. Y.,
West Shore & Buffalo Railroads.

Maps and List of Boarding Houses Free on Application.

General Office Rondout, N. Y.

H. JONES, Gen. Sup't.   F. B. HIBBARD, Gen. Pass'r Ag't

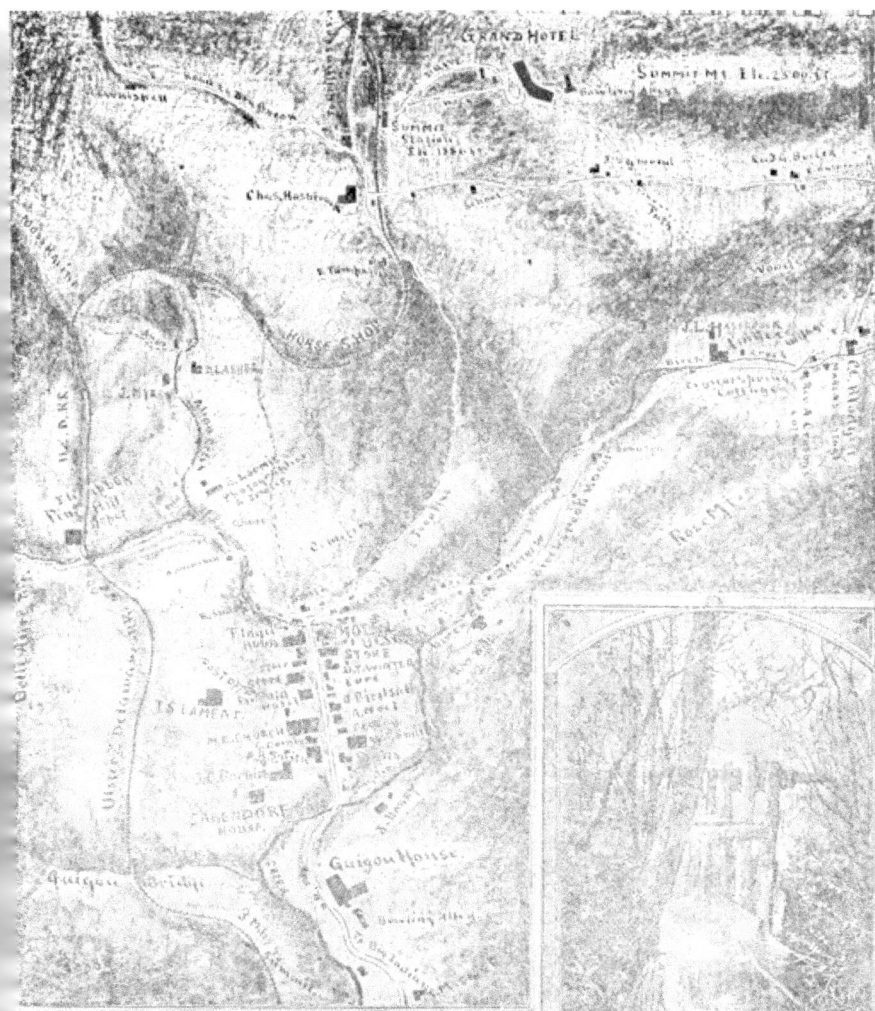

BIRD'S EYE VIEW OF PINE HILL AND SUMMIT.

Child of the Country.

CHILD OF THE COUNTRY! FREE AS AIR
ART THOU, AND AS THE SUNSHINE FAIR;
BORN LIKE THE LILY, WHERE THE DEW
LIES ODOROUS WHEN THE DAY IS NEW;
FED 'MID THE MAY-FLOWERS LIKE THE BEE;
NURSED TO SWEET MUSIC ON THE KNEE;
LULL'D IN THE BREAST TO THAT SWEET TUNE
WHICH WINDS MAKE 'MONG THE WOODS OF JUNE;

I SING OF THEE;—'TIS SWEET TO SING
OF SUCH A FAIR AND GLADSOME THING.

Pine Hill and Summit Mountain.

...

By Rev. J. Z. Butler. D.D.

THE Ulster & Delaware Railroad has its starting point at Rondout on the Hudson River, opposite to Rhinebeck, and extends seventy-four miles to Stamford. Its connections with New York are by day boats, leaving at 8:30 A. M. and night boats, leaving Pier 34, North River, at 4 P. M : by the Hudson River Railroad and by the West Shore Railroad, (to be opened in July.)

The Pine Hill Station is thirty-nine miles and the Summit Station (near the Grand Hotel) forty-one miles, from Rondout. The Pine Hill Station is 1,660 feet above the sea level, and the Summit Station 1,886 feet.

The Village of Pine Hill, a little below the Station level, is quite picturesquely placed, and its various structures are mainly new and tasteful in appearance, as within the past year or two it has come quite to the front as a Summer resting place. All the large houses and many of the smaller ones are specially constructed for the accommodation of boarders.

It is in the interest of these boarding houses and hotels, and for the information of

Trout Fishing on Birch Creek, near Pine Hill.

all persons seeking a temporary home for a part of, or for the whole Summer, that this pamphlet has been prepared ; and it is with reference to the general character of the region itself, and of the houses and hotels, as well as to the accuracy of the illustrations, both of the region and of its buildings, that I am requested to present these few words of introduction to the handsome pamphlet gotten up by my artist friend, Mr. D. F. Hasbrouck. A residence here for four seasons, aggregating twelve months in all, has given me full opportunity of forming definite impressions and opinions that may be of service to others seeking the mental rest and physical renewal which I have abundantly found.

First.—As to the Region, and its Special Attractions and Advantages.—Every frequented locality, both of the Northern and Southern Catskills, has much to commend it to the tourist and the Summer sojourner. But, after considerable experience and a fair knowledge of other sections, my judgment is clear that no other region combines so many advantages as the vicinity of Pine Hill and the Summit Mountain, in the vital matters of pure atmosphere, of widely extended, richly diversified and beautiful views, and of variety in the means of invigoration and enjoyment. For purity of atmosphere it cannot be surpassed, since it lies in the heart of the mountain mass, so that the breezes from every quarter sweep over twenty to thirty miles of lofty and wooded hills.

A simple statement as to the relative position of the included and outlying hills will indicate the character of the views and the variety of possible excursions. The hill above and west of the Village, which has many stumps of the great pines that gave name to the place, is itself an extended spur of the Belle Ayr Mountain. At its lowest elevation, where the railroad passes, it is 1,900 feet ; it then rises into Summit Mountain, 2,500 feet above the sea level. Both Hill and Mountain form a watershed, dividing the small streams, which find their way on either side to the distant Delaware or the nearer Hudson. The Summit Mountain, too, less than three-quarters of a mile in length by an eighth in breadth, stands entirely apart, in a quadrangle of loftier mountains, affording from its top a view of almost unequalled beauty, reaching, with unintercepted vision, from five to twenty miles in every direction. More than this, its peculiar position in relation to the deep valleys on either side, together with the many diverse lines and angles of eight distinct mountain masses, outlying in as many directions, change the view at almost every step, holding an appreciative observer in a constant charm ; and as the grouping of hill, and vale, and mountain is thus always shifting, the corresponding harmonious changes of light and shadow in the sky add their varied beauty to the vision. Beside the many easily accessible hill-points, with their attraction, there are brook-courses, and shaded ravines, and abundant woods, with pathways over which one may wander under the spell of a wondrous fascination.

Scenes in the Vicinity of Pine Hill.

Second.—As to the Hotels and Boarding Houses.—Under the brow of Summit, stands the "Grand Hotel" of the Catskills, at 2,200 feet elevation, with a marvellous picture to be seen from its broad and lofty portico of 350 feet in length. In and near the Village are three other hotels, two of them, the Ulster and the Pine Hill, having accommodation for boarders. The third is much the largest, as it is widely known for its successful management for many years, the Guigou House. Of the boarding houses there are eight or more in the Village, mostly new structures, erected for the purpose. Up the Birch Creek road there are four more, in attractive localities, within half or three-quarters of a mile from the heart of the Village. Below the Guigou House, on the road to Big Indian, there are two or three others, and upon the hill, near and a little above Summit Station, there are two houses. The houses are of various dimensions, accommodating from twenty to sixty boarders. As to the manner in which these Summer homes are kept I can only say that visitors generally have expressed their satisfaction. As to prices and locations, the pages of this pamphlet are designed to answer all inquiries.

I only add an emphatic word with regard to the cuts and illustrations. The pictures of the buildings tell their own story, as they are simply reproductions from photographs. Just as accurate and true, also, are the several illustrations. Nothing needs to be said as to their artistic merit. I ask especial attention to the bird's-eye view upon page 3. It is a remarkably correct ground plan of the whole region, and delineates with great accuracy the position of all the dwellings, including the two large stores, the drug store, and the new and tasteful church edifice.

Pine Hill and Vicinage.

. . .

By Rev. Howard Crosby. D.D.

THOSE tourists who know the Catskills only from their visits to their eastern face at the old Mountain House and its neighborhood, have a very meagre idea of their grandeur and beauty. The highest summits and wildest scenery of the Catskills are found thirty miles from the old resort of tourists. Windham and Hunter are full of sylvan glories and picturesque steeps, but the Shandaken Catskills form the very centre of romantic interest. You reach this heart of the Catskills by following up the stream of the Esopus by the Ulster & Delaware Railroad, which carries you through many enchanting scenes and up a grade of remarkable steepness to the crowning height of Pine Hill Sum-

Scenes in the Vicinity of Pine Hill.

mit, where the road is 1,886 feet above the Hudson. Out from Pine Hill flows one branch of the Esopus : down a narrow valley from the north comes another, and three miles below, the Big Indian stream from the south joins these two united, and thence onward the dashing water is known as the Esopus, till it enters the Hudson at Saugerties.

Where the first two affluents unite is the pretty village of Pine Hill, a mile to the southeast of the Summit, the view of which from any of the heights around reminds one of a Swiss landscape. On the Summit itself is the Grand Hotel with its glorious prospect over the head waters of the Delaware. Push up the Birch Brook Valley northward and you reach a divide near Bushnellville, whence a Tyrolene vista toward Shandaken opens on your right. Pass down through the village to the Big Indian, and then up that lovely valley till you reach the Slide, (or the Lion, as some call it) : climb that old mountain, until at an altitude of 4,220 feet, you look out over surrounding mountains to Dutchess, Orange and Sullivan Counties, with their farms and forests.

Go which way you will from Pine Hill, and you will stumble upon beauties. Beyond Bushnellville is the Deep Notch, with its gloomy path and ice-cold spring : over the Summit is the charming vale of Halcott and the wild defile of the Emory Brook : around the bold Belle Ayr is the way to Furlow Lake, a diamond in an emerald setting. Everywhere is beauty. Tourist, go to Pine Hill, if you would know the Catskills.

A Pleasant Trip to Pine Hill.

THESE last sultry days in the city have been too much for us altogether, and we have decided to take the wife and children away to the cooler air of the Catskills. Here we are on the Albany day boat, leaving the foot of 23d street, at a pretty early hour, but glad to get away. We pass through the Palisades, well known and old friends, and smile at Yonkers, a city in the country, and decide that we will not rest until we find something more like the real country than that. Away, away up the noble river, leaving Newburgh, Poughkeepsie, and smaller towns and villages behind us, till we stop at Rhinebeck, and gaze upon the distant Catskills with a feeling of relief that our journey is almost done. Across the ferry, to Rondout, we find the train waiting for us on the Ulster & Delaware Railroad, and presently begin the ascent, which is to land us after a short journey some 1,600 feet nearer the clouds than we now are. Up grade, along level, through valley, skirting the mountain foot, skimming along the creek, till it dwindles into a brook ; up, and up, the rarified air is cooling us off famously, and we are exhilarated, intoxicated by the change. Surely this is like going up stairs with a vengeance ! What place is this? Pine Hill, eh ? Well, if this is a hill, what do you call a mountain in these parts? The

Scenes in the Vicinity of Pine Hill.

Scene near Pine Hill.

grade is here 145 feet to the mile, and the Hill is about three miles long. Well done for the engine that accomplishes this feat with so much ease. We are now at our journey's end. Step out of the cars and let us look about this country that is to be our home for the next three months. The train is off, however, not having finished its trip, and we are left behind. It has disappeared almost immediately around a curve, and is lost to sight and hearing. Look, yonder is the Grand Hotel, perched upon the mountain side at a distance of one mile or so. Beautiful; white as marble and astonishingly large. Who would have expected to see such a hotel outside of a large city? We must go and visit it some day. But see! There is the train again, about half a mile off, going around a curve nearly at right angles from where it left us. That is the famous Horseshoe Curve. Watch it, and it presently disappears, making another sharp curve to the left, and, whistling loudly, stops at Summit Station, 1,886 feet above tide-water.

Just before us we see the charming valley of Birch Creek, extending straight away in a northerly direction, with farms and houses dotting the landscape, and glimpses of the water reflecting the blue sky overhead.

Here, in this carriage, we shall descend to the village; and mark, as we go down the hill, how the beautiful Shandaken Valley opens before us. We have now arrived at our destination, and will settle down to enjoy to the full, the pleasures of our vacation.

Guigou House.

Catskill Mts.

Pine Hill.

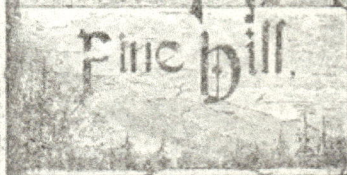

Ulster Co.
N.Y.

CATSKILL MOUNTAINS.

GUIGOU HOUSE,

Pine Hill, Ulster County, N. Y,

Three quarters of a Mile from Depot.

Elevation Sixteen Hundred Feet.

This Well Established House will Open about June 15th, 1883.

Furniture and Grounds in Perfect Order.

First class Accommodation for Two Hundred Guests.

Livery, Bowling, Billiards, Etc.

Post Office and Telegraph in the House.

For Circulars and Terms, Apply to

A. GUIGOU. Pine Hill, Ulster Co., N. Y.

—:REFERENCES:—

For the convenience of parties in New York, the following names are given:

General George H. Sharpe,	Kingston, N. Y.
George W. Powers,	8 West 50th Street, New York City.
F. W. Bloodgood,	49 Nassau Street, New York City.
Edward A. Morrison,	803 Broadway, New York City.
Rev. James M. Ludlow,	94 First Place, Brooklyn.
Jno. Kendall Dunn,	Atheneum Building, Brooklyn.
Com. G. B. Ratio, Italian Consul General,	17 State Street, N. Y.
Rev. C. W. Camp,	Kingston, N. Y.
W. Wakefield,	87 Franklin Street, N. Y.
Wm. P. Haines, (of Haines Bros.),	41st Street and 3d Avenue, N. Y.
Count Lucian Della Sala,	134 East 19th Street, N. Y.
S. Mead,	80 South 9th Street, Brooklyn.
Otto Toussaint,	120 East 41st Street, N. Y.
F. Wiebach,	84 Chambers Street, N. Y.
Wm. B. Hume,	New York.
Col. G. Thurston,	New York.
E. R. Crittendon,	New York.
F. K. Sutton,	New York.
F. Barker,	68 W. Madison Street, Baltimore.
Maj. F. Bates,	Washington, D. C.

Catskill Mountains.

HOTEL ULSTER.

B. L. RIDER. Proprietor,

PINE HILL, Ulster, County, N. Y.

This Hotel is located upon the line of THE ULSTER & DELAWARE RAILROAD. The House is new—opened for the first time last season. Is modern in its appointments—Lighted with Gas, has Postal and Railroad Facilities, the most desirable; is situated in the midst of the most attractive and Picturesque scenery of the Catskills—1,600 feet above the level of the Hudson.

ROUTE FROM NEW YORK: By Steamers, Foot of Harrison St., or Hudson River Railroad, or Albany Day Boats, Foot of 23d Street, and connect with Ulster & Delaware Railroad at Rondout.

Telegraph in the Hotel; Special Rates to Families.

B. L. RIDER, Proprietor.

REFERENCES:

Rev. HOWARD CROSBY, D. D.,	116 East 19th Street, New York.
L. M. LAWSON, of Donnell, Lawson & Simpson, Bankers,	192 Broadway, New York.
EDWARD F. KNOWLTON, of William Knowlton & Sons,	537 Broadway, New York.
JOSEPH BERNARD, of H. C. Bernard & Co.,	573 Broadway, New York.
G. BALLIS, of G. & F. Ballin, Importers,	219 Church Street, New York.
PROFESSOR SEYMOUR, Polytechnic Institute,	Brooklyn, N. Y.
C. C. WOOLWORTH,	582 Washington Avenue, Brooklyn, N. Y.
S. F. WARNER,	98 South Oxford St., Brooklyn, N. Y.

CRYSTAL SPRING COTTAGE,

J. L. HASBROUCK, Proprietor,

Pine Hill, Ulster County, N. Y.

This COTTAGE derives its name from "Crystal Spring," a cold and sparkling stream in front of the House. It is situated on "BIRCH BROOK," within twenty minutes' walk from the Grand Hotel, and one mile from PINE HILL VILLAGE, where are the Post Office, Church, Etc. In the beautiful woods, just back of the House, there are many enchanting bits of Nature and pleasant rambles. A new Cottage, built last season, could not be shown in this picture. Conveyances attend the Arrival and Departure of Trains without charge. Accommodations for Thirty-five Guests.

For particulars, address as above. See Bird's-eye View.

A few words from Rev. HOWARD CROSBY, D.D.: "For quiet enjoyment of Nature, where a kindly household ministery to one's returning wants, commend me to the 'Crystal Spring Cottage,' on 'Birch Brook,' a mile from Pine Hill Village, where my friends, the Hasbroucks, have so often given me a refuge from city cares."

❖ ORCHARD ❖ PARK ❖ HOUSE. ❖

SMITH BROTHERS, Proprietors,
Pine Hill, N. Y.

This House offers FIRST-CLASS ACCOMMODATIONS FOR ABOUT FORTY GUESTS, it was built in 1882, and is situated in a *Beautiful Orchard, about ten minutes' walk from the Pine Hill Depot*, and convenient to the Post Office, Church, Etc. The rooms are large and airy, commanding grand and picturesque views in every direction. The House is *Newly Furnished Throughout*; especial care being taken that the *Beds shall be First-class.*

Good Horses and CARRIAGES can be Furnished to Guests, desiring them, at reasonable rates.

Especial Attention Given to the Table.

For Terms, and other needed Information, apply to :

SMITH BROTHERS.
Pine Hill, N.Y.

GRAND HOTEL,

Summit Mountain, Ulster County, N.Y.,

PROPRIETORS, SUMMIT MOUNTAIN HOUSE CO. "LIMITED"

Manager, 1883, W. F. PAIGE,

This HOTEL is located on SUMMIT MOUNTAIN, in the Catskills, on the line of Ulster and Delaware Counties. Elevation above tide, 2,500 feet. It is one-half mile from Summit Station, on the ULSTER & DELAWARE RAILROAD, thirty-six miles from the City of Kingston, at which point this road is in connection with the various Steamboats running on the Hudson River, and with the N. Y. C. & H. R., E. & W. Valley, N. Y., W. S. & Buffalo and the Conn. Western Railroads.

The House will accommodate about 400 Guests. The rooms are large—and provided with two windows each, a clothes-press, or wardrobe, and all the appurtenances of a First-class Hotel.

On the premises is a Laundry, a Livery, Bowling Alley, Billiard Room, and Lawn Tennis and Croquet Grounds. Pure spring water is supplied for all purposes.

The HOTEL is a central figure in one of the grandest of Landscapes, justifying the universal expression: "No picture yet made of the House and surroundings ; no description yet written, has presented an outline of the situation as beautiful and attractive as it really is."

The roads in the vicinity are good, and the drives are pleasant and romantic.

The Hotel will Open for the Reception of Guests on the 20th of June.

Terms: $4.00 per Day :: Special Rates by the Week or Month.

Accommodation for Horses on Reasonable Terms.

P.S.: Mr. PAIGE can be addressed "GRAND HOTEL, NEW YORK CITY," until June 1st ; after that at "GRAND HOTEL, SUMMIT MOUNTAIN, Ulster County, N. Y.

GLEN HALL,

Pine Hill, Ulster County, N. Y.

The Most Attractive Locality in the Catskill Mountains.

2,000 Feet Above the Level of the Hudson River.

On the line of the Ulster & Delaware Railroad, only five minutes' walk from Pine Hill Station, and in the midst of the most attractive mountain scenery in the State. Objects of interest are reached in every direction, over pleasant mountain and valley roads.

The brooks are filled with trout, and the woods with game. The locality invites equally the sportsman, the invalid and the pleasure seeker.

GLEN HALL is a new and commodious Family Hotel, newly and completely furnished, surrounded by pleasant grounds, has extensive verandas, unusually large and well ventilated rooms; Livery and new Billiard Room, and is in every way calculated to afford an agreeable Summer Home.

Location Unexceptionable, Accommodation Superior; Prices Reasonable. Address :

H. R. CHICHESTER,

PINE HILL, Ulster County, N. Y.

Visitors from New York will take the Steamer James W. Baldwin, from Pier 34, North River, at 4 P.M., or the Steamer City of Springfield, from the same Pier, at 6 P.M. The Albany Day Boats, foot of 23d Street, to Rhinebeck, or the Hudson River Railroad, to Rhinebeck, thence Ferry to Kingston, and there connecting with the Ulster & Delaware Railroad.

Catskill Mountains.

PINE HILL HOTEL.

PINE HILL is a Popular Summer Resort, thirty-nine miles from the Hudson, 1,700 feet above tide water, and is situated at the end of the Shandaken Valley. It is, naturally, one of the healthiest and loveliest spots in the Catskills, being free from malaria, mosquitoes, and hay fever, and refreshed through the hottest weather by bracing and invigorating mountain breezes.

This Hotel has been lately improved and now possesses every comfort desirable. The Terms being very Reasonable, its Patrons will have every reason to be pleased.

The most convenient and cheapest Routes to reach Pine Hill, from New York, are the Hudson River Railroad to Rhinebeck, thence Ferry to Rondout ; Albany Day Line of Steamers to Rhinebeck, thence Ferry to Rondout ; Rondout Night Line of Steamers, all connecting with Trains on the Ulster & Delaware Railroad.

For further information, Address :

GEORGE COLE,
Pine Hill, Ulster County, N.Y.

THE SHADY LAWN HOUSE,

Pine Hill, Ulster County, N.Y.

⁕⁂⁕

THE SHADY LAWN HOUSE is located about one-third of a mile from the Depot. Twenty-five Boarders can be comfortably accommodated in the large and well ventilated rooms.

Conveyances will be furnished to parties wishing to visit any of the many charming mountain resorts, with which the neighborhood abounds, at reasonable rates.

For Terms and further Information, Address:

D. T. WINTER,

P.O. Box 27.

PINE HILL, Ulster Co., N.Y.

PRIVATE BOARDING HOUSE,

Pine Hill, Ulster County, N. Y.

ACCOMMODATIONS for about Fifteen Boarders, at a Private Boarding House. New House and Furniture. Pleasant location, about half a mile from the Depot, and near the village of PINE HILL. For Terms and Particulars, apply to

MRS. JOHN BARRY, PINE HILL, Ulster County, N.Y.

WOODBINE COTTAGE,

Pine Hill, Ulster County, N. Y.

Established in 1872.

Only one-quarter of a mile from the Depot.

A beautiful orchard in the rear of the House.

Large and airy rooms, newly furnished.   Pure spring water on the premises.

Will accomodate Twenty Guests.

First-class Beds and Table.

Terms: $7.00 and $8.00 per Week.

Address: **A. P. NOEL, Prop.,**

PINE HILL, Ulster County, N.Y.

SAGENDORF HOUSE,

Pine Hill, Ulster County, N.Y.

Summer Board near the beautiful Village of Pine Hill—two-thirds of a mile from Depot. The Telegraph Office, Church and Post Office, are within five minutes' walk of the House. The grounds are pleasant and elevated—overlooking the upper part of the Shandaken Valley.

The House and Furniture are new. Accommodations for about Twenty-five Guests.

For Terms, Etc., apply to

DANIEL SAGENDORF,

PINE HILL, Ulster County, N.Y.

BURDETTE'S HOUSE.

Mountain View House,

T. S. LAMENT, Proprietor.

This House was built and furnished last Summer, and is beautifully situated on the side of Belle Ayr Mountain, overlooking the Village of Pine Hill.

The House is three stories high, the rooms are large and well ventilated, and will accommodate about Forty Guests. Rooms *en Suite* for Families. It is quarter of a mile from the Depot, and one mile from the Grand Hotel—which is plainly seen from the House. Cold spring water is in the house. Nice lawn, walks and drives. No pains will be spared to make it a Comfortable Home for Summer Guests.

No mosquitoes or malaria. Several good trout streams are in the vicinity, and parties fond of the sport will be guided to the best places for fish. Trout fishermen should come as early as possible after the fifteenth of May, as that is the best season for trout.

ROUTES FROM NEW YORK: Albany Day Boats, Foot of 23d Street, to Rhinebeck, thence Ferry to Rondout, and U. & D. R.R., to Pine Hill; or from Pier 54, N.R., Steamer James W. Baldwin on Monday, Wednesday and Friday at 4 P.M., and Steamer City of Springfield on Tuesday, Thursday and Saturday at 6 P.M., to Rondout, from thence taking train on the U. & D. R.R., on the following morning, for Pine Hill. Carriages to and from Depot free. For Terms Address:

T. S. LAMENT,

MOUNTAIN VIEW HOUSE,

Pine Hill, Ulster Co., N. Y.

In the Heart of the Catskills.

TROUT BROOK HOUSE,

Pine Hill, Ulster County, N. Y.

Is a Private Boarding House, 1,700 feet above tide water, one mile from Depot, Post Office and Church, up the celebrated Birch Creek Valley.

TROUT BROOK HOUSE is situated between two trout streams, in a very romantic spot, presenting a fine view of the cars as they pass from Horse Shoe Bend to the Summit of Pine Hill. Plenty of shade, while the rambles cover many attractive points of interest. NO FOGS, NO MOSQUITOES, NO MALARIA.

This House is newly built, and newly furnished throughout. Veranda on three sides. Rooms large and well ventilated. Suites of Rooms for Families. Grounds spacious, and special care taken for the accommodation of Guests. Fresh eggs, pure milk and vegetables a specialty. Bath rooms with hot and cold water. An old fashioned fireplace in the parlor for the comfort of Guests.

Terms reasonable. Carriage rides to all points of interest at reasonable rates. Laundry work done on the premises. Guests remaining at the House two weeks will be taken to and from the Depot free of charge. Accommodations for Forty Guests.

C. C. BLODGET.

Pine Hill, Ulster Co., N.Y.

The Cornish House.

❧⚘☙

This House is picturesquely situated in the beautiful Shandaken Valley, overlooking the charming Village of Pine Hill, and is one of the finest Summer Houses in the Catskills. The House is new, and handsomely furnished. From the large and airy rooms delightful views are had of mountain and valley scenery. Its commanding situation affords constant breezes free from malaria; grounds nicely shaded.

The House is convenient to the Church, Post Office and Telegraph Office. To the Depot is a pleasant five minutes' walk.

Accommodations for Fifty Guests. Terms, $7.00 to $10.00 per Week, or $2.00 per Day. Good stabling for horses. Address :

J. C. CORNISH & SON,

PINE HILL, Ulster County, N.Y.

Pine Hill Village.

My House is situated three-quarters of a mile from the Railroad Station.

I have Accommodations for Twelve to Fifteen Boarders.

We are very pleasantly located, and have very fine views on every side of us.

The trout streams are but a short distance from the House, and will afford abundant opportunity to the lovers of that sport.

The Roads are Good, and Provide Beautiful Drives and Walks.

We are only a mile from the Guigou House, and a mile and a half from the Grand Hotel. For Terms, etc., apply to

A. A. MATTHEWS,

PINE HILL, Ulster County, N. Y.

PRIVATE BOARD at a FARM HOUSE.

This FARM HOUSE is about one mile from PINE HILL.

And only one-quarter of a mile from the Guigou House.

Grounds Large and Well Shaded.

There are Accommodations for about 15 Boarders

Beautiful Views, Walks and Drives abound on every hand.

Trout may be Caught in the Brook on the Farm.

☞ For further particulars, apply to

THOMAS MISNER,

PINE HILL, Ulster County, N.Y.

DAN. J. HUNT,

PINE HILL, ULSTER COUNTY, N.Y.,

Manufacturer of Fishing Rods and Mountain Staffs.

TROUT RODS A SPECIALTY.

☞ When you have the misfortune to break your trout pole, give DAN. a call and he will make you happy.

Isaac N. Weiner,   Richard Weiner

SAMUEL WEINER,

Importer of

WINES GINS BRANDIES &C

AND DIRECT RECEIVER OF

Rye and Bourbon Whiskies.

Hennessey, Martell, Otard and other COGNAC BRANDIES.
Pellevoisin, Seignette and other ROCHELLE BRANDIES.
Swan, Magnolia Leaf, Kingfisher and other HOLLAND GINS.

London Dock, Jamaica and St. Croix RUMS.
Cadiz and Cette SHERRIES.
Oporto and Tarragona PORTS.

CLARETS, CHAMPAGNES and CORDIALS.
BITTERS, IRISH and SCOTCH WHISKIES, Etc. Etc.

GOODS IN BOND OR FREE.

MANUFACTURER OF AND DEALER IN

Fine Imported and Domestic Cigars.

161 AND 163 STRAND,
RONDOUT, N. Y.

84 BROAD STREET,
NEW YORK CITY.

—PRACTICAL—

Plumber, Steam and Gas Fitter.

PIPE AND FITTINGS FOR WATER, STEAM AND GAS,

Low Pressure Steam Heating Apparatus,

GAS MACHINES, PUMPS, ETC.

40 Fair Street, Kingston, N. Y.

—•—

CONSTANTLY ON HAND

Wash Hand Basins,

BOILERS, BATH TUBS, WATER CLOSETS, &c., &c.

——Special Attention Given to——

SUMMER HOTELS AND COUNTRY HOUSES.

Guigou House

Catskill Mts.

Pine Hill

Ulster Co. N.Y.

D.F. Hasbrouck Del.